P

M000219771

When We Talk of Stolen Sisters

"I've read these poems to everyone I've spoken with recently. Mehta's immense attention to detail in diction and form, tokens of homage to other artists, and ability to write in diverse voices and styles shows how much education, experience, and deep care Mehta has invested into these poems. The poet and the poems have book smarts *and* street smarts, and that combination makes this collection completely *uncontainable*—the word that struck me most in its namesake poem, six poems in, and provided an underlying sense of empowerment throughout the rest of the collection. Mehta overflows with life, and we are lucky that the spillage produced these poems."

—Linzi Garcia, author of *Thank You*

"The poems in this collection by Jessica Mehta are visceral, sensual, and raw, built from language that is unafraid to split open and show its entrails, to display the muscle of the heart that makes it tick. With arresting imagery and deft wordplay, Mehta wrestles with the demons of loss, death, body image, aging, eating disorders, and the complexity of relationships with lovers, parents, and one's self. Like the children in 'Odense Zoo,' readers will come to these poems with 'Fingers creeping/over eyes, but still,//they couldn't look away.' In a heart-rending exploration of what it means to come to terms with self loathing and one's identity, Mehta's speaker emerges with 'a strengthening spliced in sorrow.' Within these poems, bones crack and wings rise from shoulder blades as the poet proves to us and to herself that 'it's a lovely thing/to face your fragility and still take flight.'

—Brittney Corrigan, author of *Breaking* and *Daughters*

"This collection is worth re-reading because every poem can be appreciated on so many levels. My first reaction to each is a visceral, emotional one, but re-reading allows me to appreciate the brilliance of their construction, and the third reading teaches me something deeper about Mehta that helps me learn something about myself. Poems that dare to be this open are a testament to the conviction that human connections come from a willingness to be known. Mehta's courage, over and over, to reveal her true self makes reading her work feel like discovering someone who has been a friend for decades and remembering how much you deeply admire her."

—Benjamin Gorman, author of *When She Leaves Me*

When We Talk of Stolen Sisters

New and Revised Poems
by

Jessica Mehta

Contents

Preface

I'm often asked when I first knew I "wanted" to be a poet. It's a common question for all poets, and I have no idea why. I never "decided" I wanted to be a poet; I just simply *was*. Am. Poetry has long been my best form of communication. I have poems I wrote when I was six years old. There are times I need, on every basis including physical, to write rather than to speak, and usually these writings are in the form of poetry.

Here's what I love about poetry: There's no fat. I suppose there is ample fluff in some poetical works, but for me poetry is simultaneously so lean and multi-layered, it seems there is no beginning or end—a veritable ouroboros of words on paper.

This book is a collection of new poems coupled with some revisited (and some largely revised) poems of the past. Don't be fooled by the publication dates in the acknowledgements. Many of the earlier poems were written years if not decades before they were published, and this is mostly for the reasons you may assume. There was a time I fell into the clutches of the idea that I'm only writing for myself, right? Who needs the validation of publishing? Validation aside, here's the reality: We *all* need poetry.

I fell in love with Sylvia Plath because it was the first time I realized there was someone like me out there. Or had been, at least. Someone who thought like I did, down to the dirtiest bits. She showed me I wasn't alone. Maybe a poem of mine will do that for someone else, I don't know. I still somehow don't get that there are people like you reading these poems.

So, here it is. All my insides spilt forward from dates so long ago I can't even recall all the way through a pandemic. Maybe you'll see growth on my part. I hope so. Maybe you'll easily be able to see the influences and milestones that informed these works and they'll resonate with you. Maybe you'll see yourself in there because, really, we are all part of the same whole. Sometimes it doesn't feel that way, but it's true. Look for me in this book and perhaps you'll find yourself.

These are strange days,

   the world mourning as one—all my
life heart
breaks were solitary
pursuits and now, naked
   streets wail back
at the vacuum roaring
inside. We panic by:
arms pregnant with moly,
   snowy softness
bring us back
to mama's arms (remember,
at one time, someone loved us)
   more than their own skin   breath
       every
thing we've ever hunted
and howled for is slipping
off shaking shelves. When did   home
   get so keeningly lonesome to bear? When

we started waking up. Look, just look—
look at all the beautiful.

When we talk of stolen sisters

we talk of bodies gone to ghost
or given back for goodness—as if

we are

sweets snatched from superettes
discovered post-wash in sticky pockets.

When we think on stolen girls

we imagine
pluckings from roadsides,
                              wild

flowers wafting honey-sick. Passed 'round,
stuffed in vases to wilt,
before given back to ground.

When we hear of stolen daughters

we listen
with colonized minds. Settle
into armchair arguments,
share, shake heads, repeat.

When we read of stolen women,

we say,

But it's not me, my cousin,
my child, my life—not really
(until it is). When they speak

of taking us

it's not an outing, a going,
a coming back 'round again.
Stolen implies ownership, so

who then owns these sisters?

And I Did Eat

Like any good atheist, all I do is write[1]
about God. Malum to malus,
Eve was the first disorder-

ly eater.[2] Behold the riches
of the body. The fig is no
fruit gleaming, a crowning

jewel birthed between folds

of her hallowed self. Taste the unraveling
of this inverted flower, filled
with male lovers of paper
nests ... tucked

stings and crawling hope.
Blossomed unto openings,
they are blind,
flightless. Incestuous. Desperate.

---

[1] The opening line is in reference to a letter by Sylvia Plath to "Father Bart" dated 21 November 1962 in which she writes, "I am myself, ironically, an atheist. And like a certain sort of atheist, my poems are God obsessed, priest-obsessed. Full of Marys, Christs and nuns."

[2] The line "Eve was the first disorder- / ly eater" is inspired by *Deprivation and Power* by Patricia McEachern in which she writes, "The first woman was the original and quintessential disorderly eater" (pp. 1).

(A burrowing to freedom—pardon
the egress.) A woman loves
a woman, starving

in traps, sure
in this undoing. Inter-
petals open, ripen
for my lips.

What have I done?

Lady,
you beguiled me

and
I
did
eat.

To(o) Intimate

To intimate is to suggest I shouldn't (perhaps)
tell you *Give me prayer hands* (*higher*)
so ropes don't lash your face (bottoms, you see,
don't want rope burns on *those* cheeks
unless they ask for it
specifically). It's too intimate, they said,
using measuring tape
instead of hemp hank. I suppose
it's fine when doctors   family
      loved
ones   friends   that one
celebrity   the blogger on IG
tells you you're the wrong kind
of thicc but inch by inch in *real life*
is too triggering for some. I'd like
to intimate, yet again, that *this*
is not mature/adult/triple-ex ex ex content,
this
is the human body   canvas   form
un-sheathed and, anyway, *Does this look*
sexual to you?[3] Nudity is to intercourse
and averted eyes as books are to madness
and mutiny. It's too intimate to intimate
that we are beautiful stripped and hog-

---

[3] The line *Does this look / sexual to you?* is from the film *The Secretary*

8

tied in public. Let me paint my experiences
in cinema red across crowning iliac
crests and count the seconds dripping fast
before they shut us down in shameful protest.

The Body of Cat

His ashes arrived on a Sunday, god's
day, mid-pandemic deep. Fitting—
his eyes once cradled
galaxies spilt over. I took my eucharist

at noon, fingertip of ash and bone.
He tasted nothing
like how he'd lived. Silt to tongue,

take this, for this

is my body. I remember limbs
gone stiff, sticky rose
lickings down my arm. Drink,

child,

for this is my blood—thicker
than morning
purrs. Now,
I carry him
within me, his sighs ballooning
my soul. I do not know yet

(but I pray) …

may he imbue me something beautiful:
a strengthening spliced in sorrow.

Uncontainable*

My body gleams the same
shining cost
as a new car. Gilded in gold.
Punctuated in gems. You ask,
What would your mother think?
(she thinks nothing, she
is dust, but)

if she were to rise up, gather
her ashen self once more, then

I say,

she'd delight in my adornments, diamond
'round daith, topaz to tragus. Trace
these inky birds sprung from skin
(even the one who lied,
 I love you),[4]
to nest in lion's den and say,

Our bodies are no temples

---

[4] *The line, "even the one who lied / *I love you*" is inspired by the opening
paragraph of Toni Morrison's *Jazz* which reads, "She ran, then, through
all that snow, and when she got back to her apartment she took the birds
from their cages and set them out the windows to freeze or fly,
including the parrot that said, "I love you."

> *to keep*
> *and sweep pristine.* Make of that

fragile shell

everything

you dream. Draped in colors, dripped
in stones shaken from earth so when
we return, fragmented super-
nova, we can say,

Recall, that once-was canvas,
Icarus footprints burned
to brown and all
the blinding beauty it spilt forth—
uncontainable.

Uncontainable.

The Seeds for Distinction*

Conductor drives us, the cow-
   catcher barreling straight into the teeth
   of Memory's harshest winter.
      Derailed and steam
      rolled, Igitsi's tears trail
         to track, past the seeds
            sewn into skirt to crack
               like a spoon against Colonel's
               crème brûlée. Add salt
            to taste. Fold into the earth, let
         rise a route of roses—ivory corollas
      birthed from all the gold
   they couldn't take. Conduct yourselves

         like noble

   savages.[5] Conductor raises
      his baton. March to the beat
   of nettle across neck, *Cadenza,*

---

[5] *Prior to Thomas Jefferson's presidency, he was a Colonel of the
Albemarle County Militia. He was later credited with starting the Trail of
Tears. Jefferson dubbed Native Americans "noble savages" and also called
for a "need for [Native] extinction." The various routes taken during the
Indian Removal Act, of which my direct ancestors survived, were overseen
by white "Conductors." The women sewed bean pole seeds into the hems of
their skirts and dresses, and the Cherokee Rose is said to have sprouted
along the trails from the women's tears.

cadenza! We are

not the removed, we are

the Movement—largo
to grave—a whole orchestra
of virtuosos with drumming
chambers keeping cadence.

To Dear Sir

Sir, hinder what I've done. I was once tied
to metal bed legs so long nerves
were severed and I've never held
a pencil right since. Sir,
render me one same piece

once again, my parts

are littered all behind me. Sir, Ender is coming—
they're on my dissertation panel,
the doctors with biopsy tubes
lined up neat as soldiers, the husband
who's seen my insides are fermented
in fear. They say, *Sir, end her suffering,
(like a dog.)* Kafka rolls or shakes and his
will be the last words sloshing
in my broken head. I surrender

to it all, your price tags, the everythings
I knew were arriving—slow and seasick
like heirlooms shipped in bubbles.

Prey Better Pray

Next time that corner man
say, *Smile girl!* remember the vast
majority of predatory mammals
    show
        teeth
as a warning. Next time a gas
station attendant asks what you got
to be so sad about, you go on,
stretch on that beauty queen grin,
Vaseline thick as fine thighs
on those canines 'cause
they oughta know
    prey
        better
            pray. I been told
too many times, there ain't nothing
to be sad about, what I got
to be depressed for, anyway?
What's wrong? You ain't got
no man? I could make you
smile so good or you one
of them stuck up bitches think
you better than all this?
Got a home, a hot little ass,
could have 'em crawling
on them preacher soft
thin-skinned bellies like salamanders

if I'd wanna. *Little miss,*
  you could be

    so pretty
      if you tried. Try

and know this: They're asking
for it, all of 'em. Go on then,
show 'em, spread out
    all
        you
              got—
that good stuff, sharp stuff
clean 'n glistening on velvet.

The Heart Consumes Itself

It's not true the starved
don't eat, we die

of broken hips, pelvis
churned to dust—slowly,

the heart consumes
itself. Atrophies and implodes.

      (These chambers, remember,
are a muscle.)

Nobody nowhere shoulders
the strength to stop it all, the whole
fat world from slipping
between cracked, wanting lips. We eat

and we hate,

with each bite and gag-
me spoon. Our weakness
displayed like limbs
splayed wide, flushed
shameful folds of pink.
How I wish

I could stop. Let the valves

shut down cold. Listen,
that last organ coda. And you
in dutiful ovation.

Braiding

The morning of my mother's death
call, I couldn't plait my hair—a weaving,
daily habit I thought branded into cerebellum
had left me quick as her. It's fragile,
memory encoding. Ripe for damage.
Even consolidation isn't a given.
We imagine: we could eat

in the dark if we had to, the slopes
and secrets of our favorite lover. I cried
silent in the bathroom, thin strands
laced crooked through convulsing fingers
at the impossibility of it all. It had been decades
since I'd sat cross-legged between her knees
buried in shag carpet. Patient, quiet
while she wound cornrows like crop circles
along my scalp. The smell of Pert shampoo,
the snap of red rubber bands, everything
came whooshing back.

But not the braiding,

the fast fingers. Makes sense. Remember:
the heart is a muscle, too. Its memories
vulnerable to paralysis like every other run
down part of us. Still, only in stillness,
can the dead pass through, clean
the kitchen and leave us
to mop the floors of drying curls.

Should Whiskey Write a Love Letter Back

I love whiskey, adore
everything about it. The ritual,
my favorite dense tumbler, the taste
that brings me back to nineteen. All the bad
decisions rolled
up neat as tombstones. I'm here
for the scent of tar still clinging dumb
to vinyl stools. For the dim
and the din only the last bar
in town without a television
can muster. I love it enough to be whole
with one, some nights need it
to fill me all the way up. When the tour guide
in Lynchburg told us,
with the strong stuff,
you hug the amber in your mouth

along your tongue
for six seconds,

it all made sense. My apex
can tame that wandering,
my body the wild
my parents birthed into me, the root
of all my best failures. It asks less
than a winning bull ride,
this feral purring down my throat.

All the Ways

Know that

just because we're quiet
doesn't mean we aren't railing inside.
We ate herring in red coats and I told you
all the ways I'd kill myself, how
your lips were wilder than the moon.
It's a lie

that we're born alone, die alone.
We arrive

through slick thighs,
wet bellies, and maybe
we'll never see our mothers again. Maybe
she'll stick to us like burned
batter all our lonely lives. And we'll die

with all those lovers, gone
mothers, animals that licked our hurts
knotted like stowaways
in the most secret,
desolate chambers of our hearts.
They escort us, shaking

straight into the luminous.

Dawn and Death in Stratford

I never held a dying thing
until today. The pigeon
I scooped from the roadside, neck
long and shattered. Whispering reassurances
to slow-blinking eyes, I cradled the broken

body in the park while life spiraled
to empty. Barely dawn, there wasn't

emergency vet services or anyone
to watch me
carry the body in a split-open
Ziploc bag. Afraid to bash

the head in, worried I might miss, there was nothing

I could do but coo and usher
him to closed eyes, stillness—but I cradled
his heat heavy in my palms

all the way to daylight.

The Weight of Secrets

Secrets weigh a tremendous lot
so you have to be real sure
you can bear the brunt.

And that they're worth it—like a child
who cries something so fierce
you rock them to quiet, something
like complacency. Heavy burdens
only strengthen tendons, grow
muscles, densify bones so long
before the joints give out. I've borne

so many pinky swears they've built colonies
on my back. A dowager hump
never tells, words packed
with a blistering power my tongue
would burn to burst
before those syllables
would trickle fire down my chin.

How to Talk to the Dying

I looked up *What to say*
to the dying because words
get stuck in my hands. There's no good
answers. You died the same

way our father did, yellow
skin and lion eyes. What do you say

to your sister out

on the reservation? *I love you,*
that's it. Your husband told me

you smiled and poured
your own *Love*
you back into me

all the way down
through the wires. The voice

deep, dark and foreign
like a strangers' always is.

The Falsity of Fast Deaths

You picture broken necks quick
as wishing bones. I didn't know

the head could hang for hours, limp
and heavy as forgotten, unsqueezed
washcloths. That you still had to rush

them to the vet, nestle their little heads
like over-ripe persimmons. Cruel,

how the nearly dead are destined
to stare at the earth, the descent so slow—

welcoming black soil readying her grip
for a space spooned just for you.

Namesakes

My mother named me after her
father she hated. Like buying Papo's notice
with a fat grandchild would make up
for anything. My mother
named me after famous cowboys
then went and married an NDN
herself. Meanwhile, her own
mother said, *No*

darker. My mom named me
the second most popular girls
name in 1981 because firsts
were for good girls without
panic. My middle
name was the same as a boy
in sixth grade with greasy
nails and dirty hair so I
said it was short for Colette.
My mother was a surprise

fifteen years too late. In the hospital,
her father said, *She ain't much*
to look at, is she? and asked
the nurse to name her. The chosen
was Rita after her own
child and nobody not nowhere ever

could say a pearl was an ugly thing.
My mother named me

for a man she despised well
after his girth had gone
to skeleton and the coffin flies
went still—but still,

I thought a namesake
should mean something
good and holy like clean
slates, buried shames, and starting overs.

Thanksgiving at Midnight in the Emergency Vet Clinic

Nobody wants to say,
That was the Thanksgiving
he died. We reach

for dry hands 'round
thick tables with leaves
so barely used they're like a slice
of wayward rye lost
in buttermilk. We don't want

to thumb August
magazines slick with strangers'
sweat. Chew through cardboard
cookies while fast toenail
clips and *good girls* whisper
like prayers through too-thin doors.
For an hour

we listened to a woman wail
and keen. Her sobs rocked through membranes,
tore through pericardium. *I wanted*
to see him. Say goodbye. Tell him
it's okay, how much I'll always, always
love him. All the clichés
that don't hurt 'til they're real.

That Thanksgiving

I made a deal—a spooned-out hole
of my atrium, a space to cradle
her pain as my own. Traded my heart
for time. When our
towel-cradled miracle returned,
eyes kitten black with sticky
forgiveness, I wiped my lashes
and gripped my breath. Grateful
for a heartbeat, a shot of fur
into crate, god-bargained thankful
for another holiday we won't remember.

Bad Indian

Bad Indian, not a speaker—who gives
a damn if they beat it out of my father
in residential boarding school? They say,
"Pretendian" & an old man with creamed
blue eyes cackled after demanding my ancestry,

"Everyone's a Cherokee." I apologize

for green eyes, pale skin. It's not enough
to soften cries of "Wana'be clan!
Elizabeth Warren all over
again." Once an elder
vet spit on my wanting
cheekbones, my braids, that I didn't know
Lakota. I did not choose my skin

or the trauma curdling rancid
through my blood. We are born into creation
disasters, settled war zones, armed
with chanced defenses so forgive me

that ivory is my weapon. Poachers try
& they show teeth, dressed
in polyester & crafted altruism
but I am fast & I remember. I'm kamama, you really
think you got us all? We still roam

our land, thirteen thousand years is a single heart
beat in the whole story. I am telling you, listen:

I am hungry, matriarch
made too young. My grief's too big
to contain & like Damini I will starve
24 days to die from broken
chambers—and by god, how you will keen,
spill cracked-bone to your knees, pay
homage to my skeleton, to this bad Indian.

Pulitzer Prize Pig

Pulitzer Prize Pig spoke of what it means
to be ***** as a ***** man with a look
the look   *that* look
women were born knowing
how to read. I knew
that look   *the* look
at fifteen when the AP teacher crouched
beside my desk in the dark
while flashes of syphilis
and gonorrhea shuddered
across the projector screen. (Still, even now,
I hear the tired clicking of the tapes).
I knew the look,   saw *a* look
at eleven when grown men whistled
at my unfolding hips and high
school boys rolled Corollas
along middle school parking lots
with eyes that spider-scurried
pressed breasts. And I knew, I saw
that look,   *his* look
at four. In the bathtub, I learned shame—
I shot my father
in the eye with a plastic alligator squirt
gun and never bathed with open doors again.
Pulitzer Prize Pig sidled up close, nosed for nipple
drinkers and sniffed out my slop. Trough walls
are low, but sticky, slick beside stys,
and boars are happy with scraps.

Relativity

Cages are relative, the animals
showed me that. Gallops and scurries
from unclaimed Oregon wild
out back. Nightly, they came
for discount cereal, day-old
pastries, the scraps and crumbs
of our sorry offering. The skunks
groomed us to serve their favorites
earlier in winter, the raccoons
showed us they didn't like plates
or trays—thought they were traps,
proved they'd never miss a crumble.
The littlest ones, the babies,
the kits and fawns and joeys,
jolted with increasing confidence
towards the glass doors. Watched us
with curiosity as they feasted.
When we'd open the doors,
foots would stomp and tails shot up,
rushings fast into the darkness
because we,
we were escaping. And we bolted
from our cage
with a feral ferocity.

Great Grace and Sharp Wings

37 years old and still starving myself—how much
longer until I don't care anymore? You say,
Stop caring now, but I don't know
if I can be one of those old ladies
with limp hair and no lipstick.
(Not that this is old, it's just ...
when does old happen? How do we
simply slip into it like it fits? I'm not sure
I have the capacity to grow old
with grace or by any other means.)
Do we call fat 60-year-old women
fat-fat, or is that when plump begins?
How about 70? Or 80? When
does it all end and how do I stop
running hands over stomach
to see if today's a skinny day? My plan
is to die at 66, right before the life
insurance expires and maybe
(if I do it right) they'll say it was a slender
old woman who fell
with great grace and sharp wings
in front of that rumbling train.
There'll be no open casket, and guilt-
laden memories are kind to the dead.
(Please, if you remember, call me beautiful
in the obits and choose a photo
where my collarbones protrude like plumage).

Place Settings

I've never belonged at any table,
but I pass
the salt and looked up

which fork to use
in an etiquette book.

All my family's dead so nobody's
left that knows there's an Indian
girl with a sick head
who grew up poor and sometimes
likes to fuck women gone
and snuck into this little fête.
They don't look too close

because I got no color
and haven't been homeless
in years. Taught myself how to talk
right with sitcoms—these days,
I only slip up sometimes. Usually,
when the drinks kick in or in catching

the smell of a fellow interloper,
overlooked uninvited guest. And we smile,
tight lips coating teeth because a feast
is always better when it's free

and a gorging
always sweeter for the starved.

mURDERED & mISSING iNDIGENOUS wOMEN

A girl gotta grow up, leave the rez, & do we talk about
it? Igido called twice for bail but both were after a
Tahlequah fall & high with opioid they drove right
through a gate. Bolted up the highway—bare feet &
all—hitched a ride via lifted truck to take her far away
before 911 with, *The devil up & took the car.* Dad left
right outta jail, headed to the Pacific & gave away that
plot of Cherokee a year later. *You'da hated it* & I
probably would have.

No folks gonna talk of them gone ones anymore. They
look at me all, *Got some bless'n on y'all*—after all, no
cop has got me (yet). No reason, really. Everyone else,
the hole fam'ly, gone & sear to memory the creak of a
cell's cot frame long ago. None of y'all can fathom at
the places gonna call for me. They gone & settle
prefrontal cortex, & that seems an okay place to some.

At 15, we 3 bunked all day 4 an aged wee-jee game:
We'd all be dead by 23 and we laughed and made a bet
4 the chance. An ATV ate Ann at 18 and then a fancy
cable hung by Althea came next. Hadn't even nudged
me 4 that plan. And when death happen that way, we
can't talk any decent way.

No one talk anythin' of funeral one or two & I kept
look out for a face I knew while the Catholic father
went on & on about killin' another or you like no
difference & prayin' for both. Father, what type of
Native turn Catholic, anyway? Who tuck that in their
brain? All thru junior year, neither talk of church or
nothin'. Creator not have way to fix it, then?

Who up and say so long to that god? Why do NDNs
stand for that nat'l song? So many of us wash away,
walk away, drag and drug away and nobody's com'n
back from that havoc of war.

Some of us hate a couple, "wo," tacked to the 1st of
what we call big boys. But with Tsaligi it's fixed—
Asgaya, male. Agehya, female. Why make that "M" all
a mess, wave wide those legs & smile? It's the 1st of the
alphabet, debut of music, the call all of us made as we
slipped to this place. & maybe that's the space us
Agehya go to. The alpha, the basis, the middle of this
wasted home.

I ran away, still a kid, and my mama said *why why why*
until pills kick'd in. With my dad and sis, *Luv y'all* was
last. With my mama, I try and say I try. I try. I try.

When they ask where we went, where we go, why gone
permanent cloys & flanks so close, why holes &
channels swallow w/ ease & no one asks or even seems

to say that's strange, remember. Remember: those who are gone never go that far. We are here. We stay. To be forgotten means an agreement's complete—that's not ever gonna happen

&

Constructing Carnage

A vine was choking the pine, throttling
its trunk and creeping up limbs.
Moss grew like pubic hair on the apple tree,
reaching past the heavy fruits to the earth.
The pear tree got it hard, plowed down
to make way for the extra wide driveway.
And the blackberry bushes? We paid
under the table to have them hacked to pieces,
annoyed at the berryblood splattering
the subfloors fresh from the mill.
For all the blessings, the *Pooja*, the cookies
given as bribes to new neighbors,

you can't cover up a massacre. There's no etiquette
that lets you pretend you didn't see.
Don't you hear the old growths screaming,
see the scared deer looking fruitlessly
for their loyal desire paths? In the forest,
where we built,
really we fit right in. What looked so lovely
in the morning mist—all Oregon green
and dewy grass—was an abattoir
the whole time. It's just,
now,
we're the ones cradling the pistols,
the guillotines, the saws
with teeth like sharks.

Gestation

The sickest parts of me will always think
you wanted to adopt because of me. Imagine
a child with my alien eyes. Teeth too small
and jaw too wide. They'd be too quiet,
prone to fat, awkward
at birthday parties and chew
like a beast at their nails. Not once
would they smile for the camera,
and *Ungrateful!* would shoot
out my lips. They'd be too afraid
to think for themselves, turn
to you or me to answer the most obvious
of questions. *What do you want to be?*
Why are you so quiet? What in the hell
is wrong with you? They'd be just smart
enough to fake it for awhile, but slowly,

in time,

the averageness would struggle up
like a pimple. And I get it.
I wouldn't want me all over
again either. Is that what it is? Why you freeze
at the questions, were so unsure
of my birth control? Can you not fathom me
from the start, bear the terribleness
that dragged me, mute and shaking,
to where we are?

Down There

My eating has always been disordered,
distorted, disgusting. I willed the anorexia, you think
it really happens any other way? The researchers
point to all kinds of dumbness, call it
mental illness. Genetics. A side effect
of magazines. Does that explain being six
years old with a father who brings
Reese's daily after work? Buy my
silence, fill my mouth so questions
don't leak out? What a deal
for just seventy nine cents. How about
college, when I rounded up
like the blue ribbon judges were coming,
got so fat all women and gay men could say
was, *Your tits look amazing!* And after?
When I got all normal? Don't think
that was an accident. Baby fat melting
like spilt Otter Pops on hot sidewalks? No—
it was a reflection of the latest disapproval,
my disappointment in myself switching
dressings again. What I put in my mouth,
what I keep out,
it's all the same. Stuffing, starving, stifling
it all down. My god, what's on the inside? What's
down there? What am I so scared
to let crawl up and out with curious
fingers and blinking wet newborn eyes?

Landmarks Made of Stone

I remember when forty was old, when
I was sure I'd escape the cancer,
when I thought my mother was beautiful. Remember

when the creak of your jacket sang like whales,
your skin soft as whipped butter
and my lips a feral ground
undiscovered? We were kids,
the lot of us, allelomimetic
but thinking we were the first. Nobody
from nowhere had found such fortunes—

quick, bury it again, hands clasped fast,
fingernails clawing through dirt
before the world sees what we've found.
Together, we'll bury our gems,

stash the gold and erect a cairn
only we'll remember the shapes of. Oval
and smooth, round with river-hewn
edges. And this one,
the jagged one, the one with obsidian
stretch marks in the igneous. This one

we'll know as ours through the blindness,
the aging, the total
fall-apart of our cocoons.

Wash Rooms

That night I laid across the washing
machine for an hour to keep
the bad wiring from shutting it down. I thought—

most women would be enjoying
a raucous, machine-gifted orgasm.
And I remembered
the man I read about in Williamsburg,
the one
who rented a crawl space above a theater
for $450 a month. Had to stoop
to save his head and lamented
how he could never bring home a girl.
I thought

I could live here. You know? Here,
in this closet of a room
where my bed would quake
like a fault line and water gurgled
below hips. My body was enough

to stop the mistakes, still the beast
and turn the makings of my draperies

clean, clean, clean.

For Erin

I remember you different, and that
is how my memory keeps you. It was a stretch
before the men we chose knew us—when your hair
rappelled in sloppy knots to your waist. The years
your mother thought we were lovers, always
balled up with joints and cupcakes
while *The L Word* labored on.
Even know, in nostalgia,
going to Slaughter's isn't the same. There are no
hangover breakfasts, no monster biscuits.
No couch guys, shit-covered walls or you
making French toast in our fall apart kitchen.
Do you know,
you're the only person who's never
been cruel to me? How strange
that you're a mother now, that your child
will never know you as anything but—
still, I know. I'll remember. With the men
you'll grow old. Your hair will thin even
more, your breasts begin to favor
your mother's burden. But you and me,
us half-girls, half-women, we'll grow young
together. Isn't is lovely, that's how I'll always
see you: Girlish and flecked with freckles, not
a whit of makeup, and your smile (glorious)
with teeth that cage our history from extinction.

Nvda Diniyoli (Children of the Sun)

The scent of your moustache wax knocks
me back, an aroma of clove cigarettes
from my early twenties—the college years
when small murders of us flocked to fire
escapes in the crumbling buildings of the urban
campus. Even then I knew I didn't belong, the first
on my mother's side to go to college,
the first in my father's generation
to speak English without a whisper
of Cherokee, though he'd forgotten
all but the easies—*usdi*: small,
alasgisda: dance, *ale ayv galieliga*:
I am happy. They beat the language out
in Indian boarding schools alongside other bad habits
like lying and pride. I snuck into this life quietly,
a cat burglar, my white face tattooed
permanent into my skin, an imposter
among the golden girls and boys.
My secret I held close where all the lies
are kept, under baggy shirts and tucked
into bras, pressed close as lovers
against my speeding heart. Years later,
finding you,
it felt like coming home—the hint of cloves,
moustache like my father,
skin brown-sugared as cut chai, and Us, glorious,
Nvda Diniyoli: Children
of the Sun.

Our Descent

It was three days after a New York bombing
and the first time
you didn't kiss me goodbye. Give wishes
for a safe flight, and to me it was clear—

if it weren't for the others, you'd will
that plane to plunder from pregnant clouds,
a painful afterbirth. How neat,
how tidy, how perfect it would all be. Nobody

would know the coldness of the morning, how
you refused to even pretend
to hear me. How it was your mother
who touched me last. Who would know

how much I drank at the airport bar,
that I worried the weight
I'd put on would be too much
for a plane to bear? No one.

You could slip on the victim's
jacket, wear it real sharp and I,

I would die with a fall, full of grace
I never managed in life. I like to think
the descent would be smooth
as your skin and slow, so slow. Reluctant

and hopeful as our restless beginnings.

On Lovers

I've had many affairs, but the guilt
was scarce. A sticky, chewy sauce
that hugged my tongue too tight—
still, it never ruined the deliciousness.

It was, as they say,
worth it. Like chocolate cake

worth each calorie, good sex
worth the pregnancy worries,
your face worth all those sacrifices. I think
there's something wrong with me,
in me, something missing
or never was. How should a person feel
when they slide with slippery ease
from one warmed-up set of sheets
to the next? Worthless, worthy?
Like a slut, or swollen with freedom?
I don't know, I don't know, all
I know is this: I've taken many of you
between my legs, between my teeth
and it was glorious, all of it,
each time, every time and I will die
legs splayed and happy, unashamed
for the crematory to burn me up.

Your Grandest Regret

You began to hate me slowly,
like a child practices skin colors
and rolls *nigger* over pink tongues.
Try it first, delight
in the oil slick naughtiness,
position yourself over me and see
all the possibilities I arrested.

It wasn't as I imagined. Disgust
is better than pity (though there was a dusting
of that, too). Like the rest, for you
my bones gave way to shapes
you could name. *Acromion, ulna, ilium.* Magic
dripped from my flaws. You started to point

to my sustaining thinness, the anorexia
never fully stumbling away. To the new muscles
creeping over my body, shy creatures
monstrous in their strangeness. And you told me,

Men, they don't like thin women. Muscled women.
They like us soft and fat like their mothers. And I knew,

between the darts of hatred, intentional
forgets and controlled apologies you
were already miles away and me,

a squinting disaster in the rearview. A mistake
you couldn't sweep away or rinse
down the drain like burned milk. Me,
your grandest regret, will never be enough
to become all the everything
you always wished me to be.

Ma'am, I Am Tonight

Rare are the great moments
recognized in the making. That night
in Nashville, the rooftop,
the five of us. I watched the magic
fall slow from the sky straight
into our darkest places. The drunkards
stumbled through, the guitarist
fingered worn strings, but he sang
everything we shouted at him.
Funny,

how pregnant sadness grows
when you watch happiness
ripen to spoil. Seconds are fast
but hours so much faster. Even then,

the taste of the whiskey, the smell
of your hair, all of it was passing

and so many times over terrible
than something already passed.
There was nothing
of meaning, no milestones,
but here's what I keep:
The squeals of the swing

dancers downstairs. How Christmas
lights hung heavy as milk-full breasts. And the words,
the throat-choke melody
of "Walking in Memphis" that we screamed
into nostalgic cacophony.

Mi Regalo

There are no *I'd likes, gimmes*
or *may I* in Costa Rica. It's all
Mi regalo. Gift me. Gift me the big
coconut, the Pepsi in a plastic bag,
the roasted cashews baking
in the equator's heat. Mi regalo
gallo pinto, a machete
to cut the grass, decapitate the lids
of garden tarantula's dens. Gift me

that bus pass to Limon, take me
away from the razor-topped fences.
Gift me long days in the jungle, seven-
legged spiders suspended
above our hammocks. Mi regalo

a return flight, an airport ride
in the breaking-down white station
wagon with the cigarette-burned
seats. Gift me a standby seat,
a skim over the ocean, a forgiveness. Gift me

another chance with him.

To Grin Macabre

Some are scared of the starved, others
arch away in awe, afraid what we have
will catch. A few hover close, fruit flies thirsty
to lick up tips—hopeful
to join us. When your scaffolding
begins to show, it's not all at once.
First the bottom rung of ribs
peek out like a shy debutante. Next,

maybe your cheekbones protrude
a little more than they should, a sudden
pergola riding where baby fat cheeks
used to pudge (where the apples
once blossomed). Hold out your hands—
press your fingers together tight.
Can you see the rays? Skinny enough
and it bursts like heaven between the bars, only
your knuckles can touch. Beautiful, right?

But here's what they don't tell you: People
start falling away as easily
as your hair down the drain. Nobody knows
how to talk to a skeleton. All bones, it's hard
to work your tongue. Hold on
to friendships. Make love
when your stomach's raging in the empty.
So let us go,

let me burrow deep into the earth
where I belong and the others like me
turn in their graves, disturb their plots
to grin macabre at the newcomer.

Plots

They say women are supposed to kill themselves

neatly, like good girls. Leave no mess behind
so everyone else can go on
with minimal disruptions. No lovers left
to scrub floors, pick up brains,
pour hydrogen peroxide on crusty bits.
That's why bathtubs are so popular. Just two
slices up the wrist, *flick flick*.

Not me. Me,

I'd buy a gun. A big one. Put it
on credit and get a whole box
of bullets (I imagine you get strange

looks if you ask for a single). And
I'd wear white, all white, like a bride
or a monk. Do my hair and smear
on real spendy lipstick so you couldn't tell
where my lips started and the blood
began to lick. I'd hold that gun a long time,

my last stupid purchase. Warm it
in my palms, memorize the lines
with loops and whorls. Then,

I'd pull the trigger
with empty lungs,
and I'd want
to think of nothing, I'd try
to think of nothing but I know—
god, I know—my mind would fill,
dark like frozen chambers,
with all those heavy thoughts of you.

Kenny, In Breeding

Kenny the tiger died like Gregor, of misunderstandings
and loneliness. We like to anthropomorphize what we
don't understand,
ingredients of our nightmares and,
of course,
what we pity. Researchers aren't sure
if Down Syndrome is the right diagnosis,
but one thing is certain:

They called Kenny sweet. So bizarrely adorable
in his ugliness—squat little body and mushroom
face. Safe. Tigers,
they should be feared. We should shake
in respect at their swaying, that wild
in their eyes. What was there for Kenny
but overcompensation with kindness? Sticky fingers
grabbing at his bars and children delighting
in his difference? Whatever killed him,

it wasn't the inbreeding. Not the side effects
of his body born bad. He knew there was nothing
like him, mistook the zoo
for a circus. The cage for a freak show stage.
What aloneness there must be
when you're damned to this world with no body.
A horror body. A body like no other.
And what a gift, what lightness,

you must feel when leaving that broken shamble
behind like trash, a crumpled pile of starts
that just weren't good enough for here.

Odense Zoo

The Danes dissected a lion before
a puddle of children. Cut him right
up, pulled the hide spread eagle
in a mockery of pornography—the kids,
they reacted like us all. Fingers creeping
over eyes, but still,

they couldn't look away. *It's important
the children see*

what the insides look like, an old man
told a news reporter as his granddaughter
clutched at his trousers. What would they see
if they did that to me? Tore my insides apart
like barbeque, rutted around
in my intestines like pigs in muck, held
up my heart as a prize? Would it be
so incredible, so grotesque?
Would the children peer
between pudgy fingers and pinch
their nose at the stink? I can't imagine

I'd hold nearly as much interest,
that the outcry would be so deafening
because I,

I am not beautiful. I am not rare. I don't scare
you when you happen
upon me prowling hungry in the night.

The Road Past Cartago

I drove to Irazu Volcano two weeks
after being split open and threaded
back together. The lurching station
wagon barely making up the curling
road. Villagers hung their fresh
laundry in the fields, stained underwear
and baby bibs slapping
in the breeze among the smell of morning
gallo pinto and cow manure.
At the highest point,
I parked the choking

car and walked to the crater,
ash and sand crawling
between toes, stitches pulling tight
in my stomach. There are no guards
en paraiso, no insurmountable fences,
no signs telling you no.
Ducking under the broken
wooden gate, I witnessed the abyss
below. Sulfur makes Diego de la Haya
turquoise as a cartoon and I
crouched down like a child,
pressed my palm hard into the heat
of a wound that blossomed
as effortlessly as a Guaria Morada,
as beautifully as the last eruption,
and wished you were there.

Dead Don't Go

The dead don't go, they burrow
into our bones, worm hungry
to the marrow. I still feel
my father blinking
through my solar plexus, asking
what went wrong. The girl
I left to hang
herself, her burst of freckles
spreads malignant across
my caving collarbones. The dead
don't leave, they decay slow
and organic, looking for a home
that feels something familiar.

Nesting

I have one of you sitting
in my throat like a pigeon.
Dirty birds—

we hate them because they're like us.
When you ask,
Tell me something, the droppings
are so sticky, dusty white I can't
choke them out. My voice
has always been stifled,

after all,

it's far too crowded down there
for us all to sing at once. But know,
scrape by struggle, I'll tell
you everything with my fingertips.

You'll find my words scrawled
on paper scraps, your *somethings*
inked in permanence. They're loud,
gaudy and nakedly unashamed
in a way my voice could never be.
So let the bird free, the filthy thing

is cleaner than all of us,

and especially me. What diseases
I've waded through, infections I've borne
and disgusts I've clutched dear
to whoosh all the way
across the wild to you.

A King-Sized Ocean

Our feet still breast-
stroke towards one another. Diving
into the duvet depths, sailing against
pilled satin sheets nubbed and bubbled
from kicking, calloused feet. I'd swim
an ocean's yawn for you,
to the darkest leagues and uncharted
wetness where the frilled sharks sleep-
circle and the wolffish prowl.

The Unfolding

I don't know what's coming next,
but god, I can't wait to live it. I told you
years ago,
that I just knew—it wasn't foolish hope
or drunken wishes, but fact. You and I
are a given, just as my eyes
are grass-green and your hands too big.
What took you so long? The ride's
been idling, chortling exhaust for years
in the waiting for you. And now,
the tickets are punched,
the baggage stowed (it was overweight
and we paid for that, of course). Now we,
clasping hands over *Asks or tells*, bolt
whip fast stupid to the unfolding.

Childhood

Two memories from when I was three
define my mother and father. A bath
in the chipped tub bubbling
from generous squirts of dish
soap that dried my skin to callous. We could never
afford the real things.
The plastic alligator squirt gun, half
full. My father came in
to shave his neck, swiping the blade neatly
around his moustache. When he finished,
he turned and scanned my naked body.
I shot him in the face,
scrubbed away his searching eyes and that
is how I learned what a gun is for.

I suckled my mother's breast until I could speak
because she wanted me to. The warm milk
filled my mouth, spreading to my limbs
like a drug. I lay on her chest in their bed,
a cartoon boxing match between a chicken
and a lamb on the TV. They squealed in one ear,
her heart beat in the other. As a bell rang and the
animals
began circling, the nipple engorged
against my tongue, grotesque and huge, and that
is when I learned what teeth are for.

Years later, I watched my best friend's
five-year-old daughter
scramble to cover her mother's
chest with a blanket as the baby
was breast fed. A child finds shame
as quickly as a farm animal
gets the metal bolt to the brain.

The Sacrament

When I was five, I sat with my mother
through the cloying night listening
for the crunch
of his tires gnawing
through gravel. She kept silent,
thumbing the phone,
as I chawed
through piece after piece
of buttered toast and jam,
my gluttony of Eucharist. It was sacred,
our secret,
watchdogs in the dark.

"Passing"

I was twelve before I realized my father wasn't white,
until then I thought nothing
of his clay colored skin, eyes dripping
honey, ropes
of black licorice hair
snaking alive and furious down his back.
My breasts sprung early, hips splayed
wide, an overeager invitation
with bones pushing unforgiving
against skin, pale and quiet
as the illness. You took me to Radio Shack,
your syrupy southern drawl wrapping
like a shy gift around the words,
My wife put something on hold,
and the young clerk, not a decade older than me,
looked at both of us with blatant disgust,
loathing and a shot of envy
even I could sniff out, like a dog
or a wild thing.

Is this your wife? and my chest
was in a painful awakening of an instant
freakishly large, my hips
unable to slam shut, and you
too stunned to be ashamed whispered,
That's my daughter. The snakes went still,
but for the years I'm too sorry to take back,

the years until the cancer sucked you dry,
I felt it for us both,
in my thighs built like a horse
my lips too ripe for a child,
in every year after labor heavy year
I refused to be seen with you, I'm so sorry
I saw you
gut punched and ugly as a man.

Two Days Prior to the Burial

twenty-some years and all i have is one memory
of you—well, maybe not one but one collection
that is the same   the same
with different places and people but we just kept
acting them out over and over   remember
all those times the waiters thought you were mexican
(my skin being so much whiter than yours – white
like hospital linens or the deepest center of stargazer
lilies)
¿Qué te gusta comer? but more than that
i remember the down-cast gaze of your eyes   shoulders
curved in like damp heavy wings   jaw twitching
beneath masseter in that way all men have
of showing pain   hurt   fear   humiliation   no more
shattered ashtrays   splintered cue sticks   urine-
soaked
closets   i don't miss you   (sometimes quietly i
miss
what i wish you had been)   i miss   your strong white
teeth
before the chemo ate the bones down to nail-thin shaven
peels
i miss the decade   before i found out you didn't meet
her
at a friend's party but through her prison
writings   memory forgive me   I miss   your
accent
when I hear it in my voice say *eugene*   *guitar*

fuchsia

i miss the days   when i didn't notice the difference in
our skin
i miss the nights   you made me brown cows milky
streams
licking down the glass

En Moravia

You're in Ticos' eyes, the plumpness
of Ricardo's lips, the trapped heat of strange
men's coiled hair overgrown as mangas. The equator
sun doesn't fade memories, it pulls
your scent out of young
boy's underarms. The rain clings tight everything
I'm trying to forget. Every day
on Ruta 43, I count colones into old mens' hands
as browned and faithless as yours.

Love You More

I sent you a keychain stamped *love
you more* from my crumbling
Costa Rican hacienda. You
were turning thirty and we
had years of regrets stitched
and scarred up our arms
like teenagers in the grip
of delusion, tired dogs
after the fights.
I waited

until you caught up with me
to say I was coming back,
my muscles tensed,
fat scars ropy thick, ready
for a blossoming explosion
black as your eyes swimming
beneath heavy brow
and deafening as your lips wrapped
like a vise around my name.

The Banana Plantation

Roberto passed a joint to me with sand-
ploughed fingers in the jungles miles
above Limon while the others
did headstands inside between sips of wine
and rum from the bottles. Nobody talked
to Roberto—he was so beautiful
he stole your voice.
I didn't want to kiss him, I wanted
to memorize how shells shook
small as pinky nails from his dreads,
how his hip bones
protruded like fins. *My father*
says that the ocean will swallow
me one day. The woven hammock
chewed into my bare thighs while he perched
like a kingfisher on the porch rail
and told me how he worked
his father's banana plantation
every morning. The smoke
poured into my head as he rocked
me gently, golden fist 'round knots,
thick accent stumbling about foreign words
and all I could picture
between his rolling r's
was the sunrise
surfing ritual, pink slipping from sky.
How his chest was roughcast,

stone from the breakers. The saltwater rutted
into him, shining off his shoulders,
even when the waters let him go, even
when his feet thrust into old Nikes,
as it was time to weave
between the bushes, slipping
plastic soda sacks
over one bunch and another.

Call to Prayer

Sick with fever in Abu Dhabi, I curled
retching in my empty bed
like a cat bent
on grooming myself
out of existence, throat hairy and tongue
thick as pregnant fig. Across the sand-coated street,
an oil-black man crept across a rooftop,
one inch tall and limbs strong as ropes
to rub and knead and love another perfect
window frame on a villa swollen
with gaud and waste. If I could
dredge up the strength,
I'd have pulled that damp t-shirt with its sucking threads
over my sweat-knotted hair,
pushed your weary boxers
down my hips, bones sprouted like wings,
and pressed my bare breasts against the window,
hot as a frying pan, my gift,
my offering,
to that sinewy miniature man
with sun tearing through skin
as the loudspeaker from the mosque
blared the third call to prayer, made the men
march like wind-up soldiers, mats cradled
like tired children in their arms.

Something Sweet

Do you want something sweet?
Your toddler came at me like a bacchanal,
mouth open with desire. Imagine
being that trusting, certain
that what was placed on your tongue would please,
the sugar grains scrubbing down palate,
the ghee melting like perfection down your throat.

Kadri didn't know I called the besan ladoo *sandballs*,
that they required the perfect mix of chickpea
and kadalai maavu, that the elachi was the secret
or that you had to sieve the flour just right. All he knew

was that *sweet* was something good, that hands
were made for his pleasures. Imagine
being that naïve, the beauty in opening your mouth.

Savagery

What are you? I can see
the Indian in your cheekbones.
My skin, white as the albumin
on salmon, the only whisper of Cherokee
etched into bones begging to be birthed.
Show me your tribal card,
your ancestry lineage, proof
of Dawes Rolls in your blood.
Am I not Native enough for you?

You look like something. Something
savage and uncontained.

How I Like My Women

I like my women slight and frail, bones
hollowly light, ribcages pressed
like prison bars against the skin.
I love the women with stomachs caved in,
divots carved like ice cream scoops
below breasts pleading to melt. It's the women
with the lips like readied blisters, skin sautéed
in good genes and creams
that remind me how exquisite we are
and of all I'll never be.

The Lecture

You think I want to be here?
Listen, I was young like you once, too. I thought
of traveling the world and I did a little and let me tell you

there's nothing romantic about drunken Korean men
vomiting on your shoes or Ticos on beaches
holding your hand and sucking down iced sodas poured
in plastic bags
while they give thirteen-year-old local girls the up down.

Just listen to me: I wanted to go to Iowa. I stood
on the murderous barstools at the Yamhill Pub on open
mic night
and told roomfuls of belligerent strangers about my one-
night stands.
I read *The Bell Jar* and fancied myself Esther
& thought, you know, if I'd just been born in the right
decade
they'd have called me more beautifuil than Marlon
Brando
& I could've been high every night

or crafted the perfect suicide letter. Listen,
I've done all that and let me tell you something you
already know,

that thing that keeps tapping at your brain when you
wake up at four

in the morning, it's already started
to slip away and you better pray,

you better pray,

you at least had the foresight during one of those too-late
nights
when you were wrapping your legs around someone
whose face
you don't remember or is just too ridiculously
familiar now that you at least did something—

something—

to make damn there's *something* waiting for you on the
other end
because if there's not, if you didn't think you'd get old
like all the rest of us, that's not going to stop
the freight train that's barreling straight toward you

& it's going to smash the living hell out of everything
because it can,
because it doesn't care, because that's it's nature,
scorpion
riding horseback here & and just like you it will roll right
over
something/someone at some time you called precious
& barely even wonder at the bump
as it keeps screaming into the night.

Bouquet of the Body

What they don't tell you about starvation
is that you hunger for nothing.
The pounds drop, an exhausted mother
releasing a wailing newborn. Inches
slough away, calluses and tired skin
pumiced off with a burning stone.
I never once felt empty.
My stomach grew tauter,
crescent arrangements wilting beneath eyes
bruised and battered as wedding day gardenias
buried in creams and powders—
and my hip bones flowered,
quiet display of Asiatic lilies,
sickeningly sweet and nearly weeping
before the decay set in.

"Eating Like a Bird, It's Really a Falsity"

—Norman Bates, *Psycho*

You don't just decide to start eating again, it happens
slow,
a groggy crawl and stumble from dream.
I didn't choose to starve myself,
I didn't choose to stop. It was a cycle, my own
metamorphosis
full of Kafka leanings and sopping new wings.

Building up like an orgasm, I can't tell you enough about
the foreplay, the spots touched that got me there,
the details of the teasing
or the fetishes reveled in (that's sacred)
but I can tell you this—I woke up
in Washington Park, stomping the trails behind the zoo.
Maybe it was the humbling houses of the West Hills,
or the reservoirs spreading like spilt champagne
at my feet, but on that day

I woke with a start. Past the rose garden poached
with pale tourists, past the fountain with droplets like
singing church bells,
I climbed to the playground at the top of the hill,
slipped onto a swing and learned
all over again

how easy it is to fly. My god, it's a lovely thing
to face your fragility and still take flight. But birds,
"birds really eat a tremendous lot," so give me the fat
ones,
the thick ones, the ones burrowed down deep.
Fill me with their earthiness 'til I choke from the grit,
desperate for air, neck arching and jaw flexing,
bones slight and delicate wings.

Things Mahavira Doesn't Know

As a child, I saw a cartoon of a devout man
endlessly whisking a broom before his steps
so as not to crush an insect—never thinking
that the man was real
or that the broom wouldn't save me. Your lips
weren't meant to know flesh
but they memorized my body, every flaw
and spark. Gujarati prayers slipped
over nimble tongue and crowded
teeth, night after stumbling
night. You whispered that my thighs
were as cool, as fair as the milk
you boiled and spooned into my mouth.

Symptoms of an End

Let me take you back to the Redwoods
where we drank cup after cup
of Dutch Brothers' hazelnut coffee,
sucked the flesh from fish bones
and salty oysters from their homes.
I'd drive you again
over the state line,
my hand on your denimed thigh
while the Oregon pines shake
with uncertainty
as if they don't realize
how incredible they are,
and you ask your empty hands,
Aren't these trees big enough?

Satyavachan

Say something in Gujarati and I see you
as you were years ago, in bars
next to gargantuan women, faded flowers
suckling your youth, moving quick as hummingbirds
flashing crow's feet with a deftness
that blurred their age. Feed me by hand
like you used to, change my water for yours,
the one ringing with ice
and tell me you love me
even throughout all the changes,
after all these years.

My father told me, *Be careful,*
you have that wandering way.

Just like him, who I see in your slowness
to laugh, the oil slicks of your eyes. I chose
you, I choose
an incredible life.

Resurrection

I never wanted to come back,
not here, where the mess sloshed over
like cocktails staining pretty satined feet.
I came back for you, happy
to leave palm trees behind,
the howler monkeys on the tin roof.
Oregon is where it began, and the Great
Northwest demanded the act end here, too.
(That's always where the hook kicks in).
Moving on,
we'll leave the rain behind, the gummy
bars tired from our twenties, the restaurants plundered
and the rain-pregnant streets already forgetting
our stampeding feet. I came back
to check for a pulse, see if We
could be pulled back sharp
from the edge of extinction.
How glorious that our vitality is so strong,
alive and kicking wildly, brute
as something shot at close range
yet demanding stubbornly to live.

The Animals of my Father

A squirrel killed my father, a tiny thing
(The squirrel, not my father—he
was a Stoneclad). A prison tattoo, freehanded
in faded blue, clutching an acorn
like salvation. His cellmate needled
the rodent into my father's copper forearm
forty years ago between games
of spades and comparing love letters.
Indians aren't fond of doctors, at least
not him,
he'd only go when forced like a petulant child,
demanding to pluck out his own sutures
with rusty pliers. He didn't know
the hepatitis snuck into the squirrel's bouffant tail
decades ago, that it slipped into the liver,
doing more damage than all those December binges
when he disappeared for days at Christmas.
After he left us, after he refused to take me, laughing
I got out before you did,
he added a buffalo to the menagerie—
it looked foreign and wild, too dark
with lines wickedly sharp. The buffalo couldn't save him
any more than his new family. Even so,

when I hear the stories—my proud father,
with calligrapher's black hair
rushing down his back, falling like a redwood
in a Wal-Mart parking lot, being forgotten
at the Indian hospital in Oklahoma, abandoned

in a wheelchair for hours with tears
like currents down his cheeks, unable to move,
without words, magnificent mane fallen easily,
wounded soldiers in the bathtub basin, I'm happy

that our last words were *I love you*
and that I'll always remember him untamed,

strong and beautiful with unclipped wings.

Mourning Lights

My father visited me in a cramped
Atlanta hotel room five years
after he died. It was hours since
I took the ecstasy from a drag
queen's bra, long after I faltered
through the doors of a basement
club on the other side of the city. I couldn't recall
how I'd got there—let alone the miracle
of slurring the right address in a taxi. The dawn's
pink fingers were just reaching in, trailing
across my wailing head, clawing fierce
into bruised eye sockets. I knew him

by his force, the dramatic entrance, that sizzle
in the air. I was still coming down, but in his glory
he hovered like a poltergeist in the room, lighting
up those cheap nylon sheets and bad prints
bright as a firecracker. In a panic I stuck
my head under the threadbare covers, sure
the ghosts would lose interest, the demons
wonder at my own magic when my wan moon face
disappeared with a snap. Weeks later I found my
comfort,
my two fingers of numbness, smooth and strong—my
father
came to me as ball lightning, a phenomenon explained
by science and dismissed as nature's freak show. But I
know,

in the deepest depths of my heart,
he gathered all his essence, all his power, all
his everything to fire up my world, and I—
I hid like a coward, a shaken toddler,
his crowning disappointment in the dark.

The Temporary Nature of Being

Bedded down in the woods,
the houses rest on stilts, dangerous,
dangling like sleeping children
on top bunks. We tiptoe like gluttons
across the Cascadia faults, as if
the sweets stuffed in cupboards
and ice cream cradled in freezers are fair
trade for our lives. The experts call us
woefully unprepared as we bow tangled
heads over sugary cereal, the morning
news unable to shock. Tsunamis overseas,
floods on the east coast—we're so sure
nothing can touch us here, not in the Wild
West, never where gold rushes raged
or Martinis were birthed to lips. Forest hugs
me close, the occasional sharp thorny fingernails
tracing taut calves or hoggish spider webs
licking my face. One day,
soon,
it will all come crashing down: the West
Hills homes indie bands made famous,
the teetering decks like behemoths,
dumb and feeble scarecrows in the sky.

The Sickest Ways

I find me beautiful
in the sickest ways,
how my clavicle rides eager
over breasts like armor.
How my veins corset forearms
criss-crossed and clumsy. And the way
I love you stupid still
after all the long jumps,
the *almost giving ups* and mistakes
big as nightmares. That's something
awe-striking in the magnitude
not even this cloying illness can burst.

Night Birds

When the insomnia punches
the liver and my mind's light
as my bones, I crank the heat
and stand naked before the glass.
The disease is most inspiring
amidst the dark, when my skin
glows like a Chinese lantern
and the subcutaneous fat remnants
murmur along my muscles
like ornaments. Scattered in the streets
are regrets paired two by two, grabbing
each other tight and halting towards
hangovers and sticky thighs. But this,
this is when I'm most lovely—
when I see my shoulders as coracoids
and not splintered, used up hangers.
When my ribs are strong and dangerous
as an iron maiden, not a cage whose every bar
I've memorized in bruises along my back.
Find me
in the darkest hour and I'll show you
something so beautiful it breaks
and hides fast as a ghost
in the excruciating light of dawn.

The Butchery Date

I'm a dumb animal
staring down the butcher
block. For awhile, the stables
feel like home, the cages
like comfort. We don't realize the burn
from the branding rod is forever,

that the fire burrows down under seared
flesh and scars straight
to spongy marrow. The prods move us
forward, dirty feet shuffling
 towards the same bolt pistol ending
as everyone else. Fingernails and horns

are made from the same
thing, tough envelopes
of keratin to ward off attacks. What's the difference

between locking horns
in the bull rings and the slow
rides between unmade sheets? You'll find me
in the slaughter line of the abattoir.
You'll know me by your claw
marks on my shoulder. The stupid panic
in my eyes. That briny terror smell
shooting out my pores
and because, of course,

we always knew we'd meet here.

Recollections of the Training Days

Dogs with prong collars adjust to the pinch—
that was me, immune
to the warm blood trickles
when he petted my car's hood, see
if I'd strayed that day. My skin grew tough
against the spikes, so I got used

to the next telling me
I was *almost thin*
and should only speak
when commanded—like a dog,
a bitch, like something that scurries
on all fours tonguing up compliments
alongside filthy water bowls.
And then there was you. There are times
you make me feel like an animal

in the right ways. Times
when I need to re-learn tricks I lost
over the years like chewed
up toys or buried, cherished things.
I remember the choking nails in the deepest

of nights and how it felt
when you slipped them off, easily
and quickly
like my threadbare shirts
when you undress me in the mornings.

The L Words

I got up, still a little drunk, and ran
for miles after loving you. Sidewalks fell down,
verbs turned to nouns, at four
in the morning when I'm leaving you.
My legs stretched 'til they broke, snapped
and tore with each stroke
and the sun—the sun
grooved into soberness
as I'm losing you.

Space

As children, two oceans
separated us, the Pacific flirting up my legs
hungry as a frantic demon
on those frigid coastal trips. The Atlantic
cloyed like a diseased and desperate
lover close to your family
home in Mumbai. Twenty years ago
neither of us would have believed
it would all come down to Us—you,
a child playing cricket in the streets,
me plotting my escape from that smothering
small Oregon town, and We,
what we found was unsinkable, for good,
a buoy no ocean dare drown.

The Constellations of My Body

I flanked myself in pretty, a dressing
since I had none of my own. I was always friends
with the beautiful girls,
the Hawaiian girl, the girl
next door, the one
who killed herself. They adored me the same
as children do, toddlers demanding and wondering
why I ignored their magnificence while everyone
else fell at their feet. That's why

I tanned the cancer into my flesh, chasing
her exotic reaches, shaved my teeth
to needles and cemented on porcelain, filling
my mouth with bathroom fixtures, let doctors
cut me apart like a hunting prize
in Central America, piece me back together,
all mismatched quilt of muscle and skin.

(Even the lawyers say
I shouldn't have survived.)

My silence agreed when strangers called me fat,
when others said I was too ugly to bask in the company
of such beauteous presence, when the old queen
in London laughed, *You'll never be beautiful.*
And then there was you.

In the frozen dermatologist's room, he
taught you to sniff out the cancer,
the rough edges, the swirling browns.

Do you love her constellations? he asked,
and your silence said Yes—the stars of my body,
shooting meteors, the fallout from years
in tanning beds seen for once as gorgeous
in their danger, those remote incandescent
miracles dying bright like fireworks
in the deadliest regions of my nights.

If I Write About You

If I write about you, you're important
even if it's just once, even
if it's in passing. My love collects like coins,
fine precious metals,
in the cobwebbed attic of my heart. It occupies
all corners, each seam of every beam.
If I write about you,
I'm keeping you and nobody or nothing
can claim your space. You've become
a part of me, as necessary as my limbs,
my breath, my blood. When I write about you,
it's a testament, my shouts to the world
that in this instant, you're everything
that matters. And even if it fades,
even when it dims,
the echoes of our collision
will reverberate in my chest, play conductor
to the orchestra of my heartbeat.
Do you know what power you have,
how many blessings you're gifted,
when I play god and make you immortal,
supplicating like a peasant while you're reborn
omniscient in drying ink? I choose happily
to bow before you, grateful and obliging
to simply be here
basking in the splendor of You.

Emergency Preparedness

I've learned to roll through your storms
like a Kansan figures out real quick

bathtubs usually stay put in a twister.
For you I hung on

to the rusted pipes,
the gurgling sounds, the cool slickness
of underbelly. Our years showed me
to wait out the quiet, bear down hard,
not scramble to drown the silence
just because.
I memorized your moods—
unspoken languages are the easiest,
most dangerous to unravel. Now,
I realize when you chop up my pet names
coarse and rough into senseless Hindi
you're happy, ripping at the seams with smiles
and spilling over with touches. When you're hungry,
your skin needs a drink first, lapping up lukewarm
shower rain and Dove soap. And when you don't want to
speak,
I can't make you. I shouldn't even try. I know
how to weather the seasons, how to not get soaked
in the storms and where my secret
umbrellas of strength are kept, bundled tight
and ready to burst open with the slightest push.

The Art of Patience

From you I learned the art of waiting, the art
of patience. I thought I knew quiet,
drenched myself in it as a child, wore
it like a puffy coat well into adulthood—
when quiet breaks down, you can bury yourself
in layers of fat and bad skin.
But when that sloughed off I was left
with nothing. No quiet,
no buffer, nothing to keep me safe
from the shark-like assaults
of the world. You showed me
what it means to wait. To not speak
just to soften awkwardness, not demand
answers when they're as undeveloped
as the embryos I flushed from my body,
never regretted remnants of the lost years.
You taught me the beauty of closed lips,
the power of reticence and how to command,
thundering like a lion with my eyes.

Grooming

You clip your nails like one does a child's, I hear you
in the bathroom between the local news breaks
and trumpets from the stadium across the street. To the
quick,
toeing across the free edge, your fingernails are all fresh
cuts and uneven trims. It's here,
in these moments,
when you emerge down the hallway,
every stray piece of you swept up neat in bins, I imagine
how you used to be. Before America, when your
grandmother
would snip at your fingers carefully, dreaming up half
moons
and stories dipped in magic. Afterward, each digit was
battered
in ghee and sweet jams, plucking at parathas and wiping
up dahl. I've always adored your hands, the histories
they cup into the plunging, echoing crevices and the
empty
crags begging to be filled with squeezes and pinches of
me.

A Tiger for Christmas

When I gave you a tiger, I didn't know
he would become our Christmas tradition,
our own *little Saigon*—years older than wild tigers,
hundreds of pounds less, with a craving for hearts
of horses from the slaughterhouse across town.
Like you, he was born in a cage, the pull
of alone-dom strong as his haunches, thick
as the canines that cracked down on stallion bone
like murukku. Like you, his eyes tracked
those who stared, the passerby with heavy cameras,
the brave ones who got too close. He was ours
through his end years, past the mourning days
for his sister. He didn't pounce, didn't preen,
didn't growl like the others. *He knows
he's a tiger*, you said. And for that,
I gave him to you, a beast spilling
with killing power and a taste for tired love muscles.

When to Stay

They say I don't know when to leave, I say
they don't know
when to stay. What good comes
after the bars shut down, past the window
of *these shoes could go all night?* Knowing
when to stay is what brought me to you.
Knowing how to stay shot us
through the affairs, the culture battles, the year
I ran away to another land with another man
while you played stowaway
in my organs. When you know
when to stay, how to close
down the party and watch the lights come on,

you see everything. The way the floors
are caked in syrup and the booths
worn to threads. How the dancers
wear their stretch marks and the barbacks'
fingernails are chewed. We stayed through
the last song, the final bathroom checks,
when the last dish was scraped of tots
and plopped into the machine—through the ugly
and into the empty morning streets
where New and Hope trudge soft
and amble on bare feet into the next.

We Carry On

everything would be easier had I never found you,
but who wants a simple life? Give me the hard stuff,
the twists that leave us lurching and introversions
making hearts gush. I see the settling
all around me, comforts others cling
to like pilled blankets. I watch their thighs
expand, habits stick like sloshed batter
to hot stovetops. And it's devastating,
that slow shuffle
back to the earth. Their heads
tuck down into heavy, invisible feedbags
as the fattening season drones on, but we,
we've carried on. The two of us,

we carry on.

Pack Animals

We sleep like dogs, backs pressed
flush against each other. Pack
animals, you guard the door
while I keep watch of the closet—who knows
what monsters may appear,
which drunk neighbors might rattle
down the hall. Your body's heat
slips moist fingers over my hips, sticks
my skin to yours while we curl
in for the deep. Bony knees
and sloping thighs reach outward
like stars in our cry, our little litter,
our mute in the duvet wilds.

The Other Side

Call this a love letter, call it
Our Story,
unlike anyone else's, but with threads
and adornments from the great
ones—the star-crossed fables, the fairy tales
we craved and gobbled down as greedy
little beasts in our parents' arms. Call this
What shouldn't have been, all hurdles
and bounds through flaming hoops,
seasoned with heartbreaks and flavored
with blindfolded leaps. There are all kinds
of names for what we've done, for who
we are and where we've been.
Call it a freak accident, a liquored up
lurch into just the right nook
of just the right place. This
is called finding the great stuff
and having the thick tenacity
to hold on knuckle white
through all the blinding explosions.

Orygun

When I find myself missing
Wild, I walk for hours through the wet-
lands 'til my hips grind to dust,
mud suckling at my feet.
This is what I'll miss
when another city swallows me whole.
The deer hooves in the depths,
throaty frogs with lustful lines,
marionberries sprawling fat
and frenzied. So let yourself
be Wild. Suck the cold air deep,
rattle it around your lungs
to fog up your insides.
How blessed are we, born
into the Oregon green,
how lucky we are to carry
her ferality in our bones.

About the Author

Jessica (Tyner) Mehta, born and raised in Oregon and a citizen of the Cherokee Nation, is a multi-award-winning interdisciplinary artist, author, and storyteller. She has received several writer-in-residencies around the world which were pivotal in supporting her writing of 15 published books. She is currently the post-graduate research representative at the Centre for Victorian Studies at the University of Exeter, England. She is the first Native American to serve in this role at the largest institutional Victorian research center in Great Britain. Her doctoral research addresses the intersection of eating disorders and poetry. Learn more about Jessica at her website, www.thischerokeerose.com, where you will find links to her books, upcoming projects, and the Emmy award winning documentary on her life and work from Osiyo Television.

Acknowledgements

"A King-Sized Ocean" was first published in "Eunonia Review" (2017) and collected in *Secret-Telling Bones*

"A Tiger for Christmas" was first published in "Lily Poetry Review" (2020) and collected in *What Makes an Always*

"All the Ways" was first published in "Allegory Ridge" (2017) and collected in *Constellations of My Body*

"Animals of My Father" was first published in "The Elephant Magazine" (2017) and collected in *The Last Exotic Petting Zoo*

"Bad Indian" was first published in "Rising Phoenix Review" (2018) and collected in *Bad Indian*

"Bouquet of the Body" was first published in "L'Allure de Mots" (2013) and collected in *The Last Exotic Petting Zoo*

"Braiding" was first published in "Rising Phoenix Review" (2018) and collected in *Savagery*

"Call to Prayer" was first published in "And/or" (2014) and collected in *The Last Exotic Petting Zoo*

"Childhood" was first published in "The Cossack Review" (2013) and collected in *The Last Exotic Petting Zoo*

"Constructing Carnage" was first collected in *Bad Indian*

"Dawn and Death in Stratford" was first published in Colloquial: A Poetry Review (2017) and collected in *Constellations of My Body*

"Dead Don't Go" was first published in "South 85 Journal" (2016) and collected in *Secret-Telling Bones*

"Down There" was first published in "Urban Sasquatch" (2016) and collected in *Bad Indian*

"Eating Like a Bird, it's Really a Falsity" was first published in "Massachusetts Review" (2020) and collected in *The Last Exotic Petting Zoo*

"Emergency Preparedness" was first collected in *What Makes an Always*

"En Moravia" was first published in "Contemporary Literary Review India" (2012) and collected in *The Last Exotic Petting Zoo*

"For Erin" was first published in "Babbling of the Irrational" (2016) and collected in *Secret-Telling Bones*

"Gestation" was first collected in *Bad Indian*

"Great Grace and Sharp Wings" was first published in "Sheila-Na-Gig" (2019) and collected in *Bad Indian*

"How I Like My Women" was first published in "Collected Letters" (2018) and collected in *The Last Exotic Petting Zoo*

"How to Talk to the Dying" was first published in "Causeway Lit" (2017) and collected in *Constellations of My Body*

"If I Write About You" was first published in "Picaroon Poetry" (2017) and collected in *What Makes an Always*

"Kenny, In Breeding" was first published in "Portland Family Magazine" (2016) and collected in *Secret-Telling Bones*

"Landmarks Made of Stone" was first published in "Roar: Literature and Revolution by Feminist People" (2017) and collected in *Bad Indian*

"Love You More" was first published in "Common Line Journal" (2018) and collected in *The Last Exotic Petting Zoo*

"Ma'am I am Tonight" was first published in "Vending Machine Press" (2016) and collected in *Secret-Telling Bones*

"Mi Regalo" was first published in "Vending Machine Press" (2016) and collected in *Secret-Telling Bones*

"Mourning Lights" was first published in "Hobo Camp Review" (2018) and collected in *What Makes an Always*

"mURDERED & mISSING iNDIGENOUS wOMEN" was first published in "Eunonia Review" (2018) and collected in *Bad Indian*

"Namesakes" was first published in "The Dead Mule School of Southern Literature" (2018) and collected in *Drag Me Through the Mess*

"Nesting" was first published in "Zone 3" (2018) and collected in *Secret-Telling Bones*

"Night Birds" was first collected in *What Makes an Always*

"Nvda Diniyoli (Children of the Sun)" was first published in "The Elephant Magazine" (2017) and collected in *What Makes an Always*

"Odense Zoo" was first published in "Howl" (2017) and collected in *Secret-Telling Bones*

"On Lovers" was first published in "Vending Machine Press" (2016) and collected in *Secret-Telling Bones*

"Orygun" was first published in "Anti-Languorous Review" (2017) and collected in *Orygun*

"Our Descent" was first published in "b(OINK)" (2017) and collected in *Secret-Telling Bones*

"Pack Animals" was first published in "Black Napkin Press" (2017) and collected in *What Makes an Always*

"Passing" was first published in "The Iguan Journal" (2013) and collected in *The Last Exotic Petting Zoo*

"Place Settings" was first published in "The Pangolin Review" (2019) and collected in *Bad Indian*

"Plots" was first published in "Eunonia Review" (2017) and collected in *Secret-Telling Bones*

"Prey Better Pray" was first published in "Glint Literary Journal" (2019)

"Pulitzer Prize Pig" was first published in "Pennsylvania English" and collected in *Bad Indian*

"Recollections of the Training Days" was first collected in *What Makes an Always*

"Relativity" was first published in "The Lake" (2017) and collected in *Bad Indian*

"Resurrection" was first collected in *The Last Exotic Petting Zoo*

"Satyavachan" was first published in "Fearsome Critters" (2018) and collected in *The Last Exotic Petting Zoo*

"Savagery" was first published in "Anti-Languorous Review" (2018) and collected in *The Last Exotic Petting Zoo*

"Should Whiskey Write a Love Letter Back" was first published in "Subprimal Poetry Art" (2017) and collected in *Constellations of My Body*

"Something Sweet" was first collected in *The Last Exotic Petting Zoo*

"Space" was first collected in *What Makes an Always*

"Symptoms of an End" was first published in "A Clean, Well-Lighted Place" (2012) and collected in *The Last Exotic Petting Zoo*

"Thanksgiving at Midnight in the Emergency Vet Clinic" was first published in Structural Damage (2017) and collected in *Drag Me Through the Mess*

"The Art of Patience" was first collected in *What Makes an Always*

"The Banana Plantation" was first published in "Speculative Edge" (2012) and collected in *The Last Exotic Petting Zoo*

"The Butchery Date" was first collected in *What Makes an Always*

"The Constellations of My Body" was first published in "The Real Us" (2016) and collected in *What Makes an Always*

"The Falsity of Fast Deaths" was first published in "Eunonia Review" (2017) and collected in *Drag Me Through the Mess*

"The Heart Consumes Itself" was first published in "Fearsome Critters" (2018) and collected in *Savagery*

"The Lecture" was first published in "Furnicular Magazine" (2018) and collected in *The Last Exotic Petting Zoo*

"The Other Side" was first collected in *What Makes an Always*

"The Road Past Cartago" was first published in "Cold Noon Poetics" (2012) and collected in *The Last Exotic Petting Zoo*

"The Sacrament" was first published in "Flycatcher Journal" (2013) and collected in *The Last Exotic Petting Zoo*

"The Sickest Ways" was first collected in *What Makes an Always*

"The Temporary Nature of Being" was first collected in *What Makes an Always*

"The Unfolding" was first published in "Structural Damage" (2017) and collected in *Secret-Telling Bones*

"The Weight of Secrets" was first published in "Really System" (2018) and collected in *Drag Me Through the Mess*

"Things Mahavira Doesn't Know" was first collected in
The Last Exotic Petting Zoo

"To Dear Sir" was first published in "Quiddity" (2018)

"To Grin Macabre" was first published in "Allegory Ridge"
(2017) and collected in *Secret-Telling Bones*

"Two Days Prior to the Burial" was first published in
"Glint Literary Review" (2012) and collected in *The
Last Exotic Petting Zoo*

"Wash Rooms" was first collected in *Bad Indian*

"We Carry On" was first collected in *What Makes an
Always*

"When to Stay" was first published in "REaDLips Press"
(2017) and collected in *What Makes an Always*

"Your Grandest Regret" was first published in "Vending
Machine Press" (2016) and collected in *Secret-Telling
Bones*

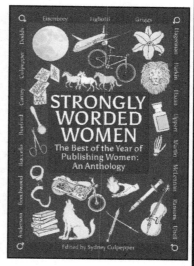

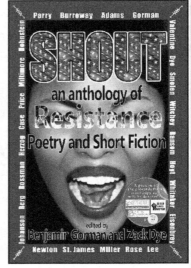

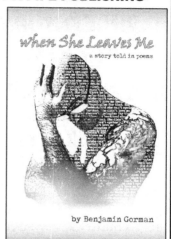

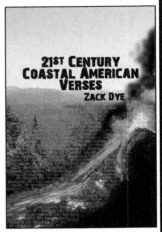